BASEBALL

WHO DOES WHAT?

BY RYAN NAGELHOUT

Gareth Stevens
PUBLISHING

Please visit our website, www.garethstevens.com. For a free color catalog of all our high-quality books, call toll free 1-800-542-2595 or fax 1-877-542-2596.

Cataloging-in-Publication Data

Names: Nagelhout, Ryan.
Title: Baseball: who does what? / Ryan Nagelhout.
Description: New York : Gareth Stevens Publishing, 2018. | Series: Sports: what's your position? | Includes index.
Identifiers: ISBN 9781538204092 (pbk.) | ISBN 9781538204207 (library bound) | ISBN 9781538204108 (6 pack)
Subjects: LCSH: Baseball–Juvenile literature.
Classification: LCC GV867.5 N34 2018 | DDC 796.357–dc23

First Edition

Published in 2018 by
Gareth Stevens Publishing
111 East 14th Street, Suite 349
New York, NY 10003

Copyright © 2018 Gareth Stevens Publishing

Designer: Sarah Liddell
Editor: Ryan Nagelhout

Photo credits: Cover, p. 1 Joseph Sohm/Shuttestock.com; jersey texture used throughout Al Sermeno Photography/Shutterstock.com; chalkboard texture used throughout Maridav/Shutterstock.com; pp. 5, 26 Eric Broder Van Dyke/Shutterstock.com; p. 7 Rich Schultz/Contributor/Getty Images Sport/Getty Images; p. 8 Donald Linscott/Shutterstock.com; p. 9 Bull's-Eye Arts/Shutterstock.com; pp. 10 19, 23, 27 Aspen Photo/Shutterstock.com; p. 11 Ahturner/Shutterstock.com; p. 13 Rob Carr/Staff/Getty Images Sport/Getty Images; p. 14 Jamie Roach/Shutterstock.com; p. 15 Dario Vuksanovic/Shutterstock.com; p. 16 alens/Shutterstock.com; p. 21 Yehuda Boltshauser/Shutterstock.com; p. 24 karamysh/Shutterstock.com; p. 25 Ronald Martinez/Staff/Getty Images Sport/Getty Images; p. 28 Robert J Daveant/Shutterstock.com; p. 29 tammykayphoto/Shutterstock.com.

Printed in the United States of America

CPSIA compliance information: Batch #CS17GS: For further information contact Gareth Stevens, New York, New York at 1-800-542-2595.

CONTENTS

Words in the glossary appear in **bold** type the first time they are used in the text.

KNOWING THE GAME

Baseball is a game that changes with every pitch. A ball here or a strike there can change the game in an endless variety of ways. What should a player in the field do when a ball is hit to the outfield with runners on base? What should the runner on base do? With so many possibilities, how does a player know what to do on each play? They have lots of practice!

Ballplayers know their positions because they learned how to play the game when they were kids and worked hard to become great players. But it's never too late to learn how to play baseball!

BASEBALL ORIGINS

No one knows exactly how baseball was invented. It's believed baseball's rules came from two English sports, cricket and rounders. But the rules and number of players on the field changed many times over the years. Eventually, they settled on nine innings, or periods, and nine players for each team.

THERE ARE LOTS OF THINGS TO KNOW ABOUT BASEBALL, BUT IT'S AN EASY SPORT TO LEARN. READ ON TO LEARN ABOUT "AMERICA'S PASTIME"!

BATTER UP!

There are nine positions on a baseball field, and each one is different. But the one thing every baseball player must do at some point is bat! Hitting is a hard part of the job because everyone on the other team is working to stop you from getting hits and reaching base.

The most important thing a hitter can do is see the ball. They watch either the ball itself or how a pitcher stands to figure out what kind of pitch is being thrown, which we'll get to later. Getting a good swing on the ball is the best chance a batter has to get a hit.

LIVING WITH FAILURE

Batting comes with a lot of failure. Even the best hitters in the major leagues only get a hit in three out of 10 at-bats. But don't worry—much of this failure is because the other team's players are good at their jobs! Pitchers trick batters into swinging at bad pitches, and good fielders catch well-hit balls for outs.

GOOD HITTERS HAVE LEARNED TO ACCEPT GOING A WHILE WITHOUT A HIT. YOU JUST HAVE TO KEEP TRYING!

DEFEND THE ZONE

The strike zone is the area above home plate and in front of the catcher that a pitcher tries to throw the ball through. When a pitch goes through the strike zone, the **umpire** calls it a strike—whether the batter swings at it or not. Any time a batter swings at a pitch and misses, it's also a strike.

Good batters defend the strike zone, swinging at pitches in the zone while not swinging at pitches outside the zone that will be called balls. Batters don't want their hits caught or to get three strikes at the plate. Those are outs, too!

WORKING WALKS

Not every plate appearance can end in a hit. Sometimes, the best thing a batter can do is get four balls and work a walk. If a pitcher is missing the strike zone, don't swing at the ball! Force the pitcher to throw a strike. If they can't, you get to go to first base on a walk!

AN INNING IN BASEBALL GIVES BOTH TEAMS A CHANCE TO BAT UNTIL THE DEFENDING TEAM RECORDS THREE OUTS. THERE'S NO TIME LIMIT TO HOW LONG A GAME CAN TAKE!

HOME	INNING	GUESTS
03	2	00

| BALL | STRIKE | OUT | H | E |

ON THE BASES

A hit is registered when a player puts the ball in play between the foul poles and reaches a base before they can be thrown out. There are four different kinds of hits: singles, doubles, triples, and home runs. The base a batter ends up on **determines** what kind of hit it is.

Players are called runners when they're on base. Runners must be careful when they leave bases, or they can be tagged out. Some batters will hit the ball away from runners so they can move along the bases. If base runners can tell where a ball is hit and don't get tagged out, they reach home and score!

SOME SOFT HITS THAT DON'T LEAVE THE INFIELD ARE CALLED BUNTS. BATTERS PUT THEIR BATS IN THE STRIKE ZONE WITHOUT SWINGING! BUNTS ARE OFTEN MEANT TO MOVE RUNNERS ALONG THE BASES, BUT THE BATTER IS USUALLY THROWN OUT!

SCORING RUNS

Scoring runs is how you win a baseball game. When a hit lets a player on base reach home, the hitter has earned a run batted in (RBI). Players good at driving others home are often put in the middle of the lineup, so hopefully runners are on base when they come up to bat.

THESE ARE THE FOUR HITS A BATTER CAN GET. WHEN A BATTER HITS A HOME RUN WITH RUNNERS ON EVERY BASE, EVERYONE SCORES, AND IT'S CALLED A GRAND SLAM!

GET SOME HITS

DOUBLE
A HIT WHERE A BATTER ENDS UP ON SECOND BASE

TRIPLE
A HIT WHERE A BATTER ENDS UP ON THIRD BASE

SINGLE
A HIT WHERE A BATTER ENDS UP ON FIRST BASE

HOME RUN
A HIT THAT CLEARS THE CENTER FIELD FENCE OR LETS THE BATTER CIRCLE ALL FOUR BASES

THROWING HARD

A pitcher's job is to throw strikes and get the other team's batters out. Oftentimes, they do this by throwing the ball hard. Major league pitchers can throw a baseball more than 100 miles (161 km) per hour! This is called a fastball.

Pitchers have other pitches they can use to trick batters to swing and miss. A curve ball dips and drops through the strike zone. A changeup is a pitch that looks like a fastball, but is thrown much slower. This makes a batter swing too early! Pro pitchers have many different pitches they can throw for strikes!

DIFFERENT KINDS OF PITCHERS

There are even different kinds of pitchers! Strikeout pitchers mainly try to throw the ball past batters to strike them out. Ground-ball pitchers get batters to swing at pitches and hit grounders to infielders, who throw them to first base for outs. Fly-ball pitchers try to get batters to hit lazy fly balls to outfielders.

MO'NE DAVIS WAS A STAR DURING THE 2014 LITTLE LEAGUE WORLD SERIES, PITCHING FOR HER TEAM FROM PENNSYLVANIA.

PITCH AND CATCH

How does a pitcher decide what pitch to throw? They work with the catcher to figure out what pitch works best with each batter. Catchers "call" the game from behind the plate. They **crouch** down behind the plate and use different fingers to signal to the pitcher what they should throw.

Catchers need to keep pitches from getting behind them. Sometimes the catcher will block a **wild pitch** in the dirt or have to throw to second base on a **stolen base** attempt. They also have to tag out batters trying to score by reaching home! It's a busy job!

Catchers are smart and **athletic**. They often watch film of batters with their pitchers so they know what pitches batters like to hit and what they struggle with. This kind of studying might even include lots of math. They need to know the opposing team's hitting **statistics** to know how to keep them from scoring runs.

TOGETHER, A PITCHER AND CATCHER ARE OFTEN CALLED A BATTERY. THEY WORK TOGETHER TO GET THE OTHER TEAM'S BATTERS OUT!

15

WHO'S ON FIRST?

Every position in baseball is important, but the first baseman might be the busiest of all the position players. The first baseman's job is to catch any ball a teammate may throw their way to get a batter out. Defensive plays on soft-hit ground balls often end with an infielder throwing to the first baseman.

The first baseman puts one foot on the base, then leans toward the person throwing the ball and catches it as soon as possible. If the ball reaches their glove and their foot is on the bag, or base, before the batter reaches the base, it's an out!

NICE CATCH, LEFTY!

What hand you throw with matters in baseball! Left-handed throwers often play first base because they don't have to make tough throws to their left, which is harder for a lefty to do. First basemen who wear their glove on their right hand also can field balls hit between first and second base easier from the position.

FIRST BASEMEN CAN ALSO SNAG HIT BALLS BETWEEN FIRST AND SECOND BASE, THEN STEP ON FIRST BASE FOR THE OUT. THIS IS CALLED AN UNASSISTED OUT BECAUSE IT WAS RECORDED BY JUST ONE PLAYER!

THE MIDDLE INFIELDER

Unlike the first baseman, second basemen don't spend much of their time at second base! They play between first and second base and wait for balls hit in play between the bags. They often make diving stops of balls and throw them to first base for outs. Second basemen need to be able to cover a lot of ground.

Sometimes, they'll go to other bases to field throws made by other players. Second basemen can cover second base to get a runner on first out on a hit in play. Sometimes, they'll then throw it to first base to get the hitter out, too. That's a double play!

TURNING A DOUBLE PLAY TAKES FIELDERS WORKING QUICKLY TO GET THE BALL TO TWO BASES BEFORE THE RUNNERS REACH THEM. "TURNING TWO" IS A VERY EXCITING PLAY!

ARM ON THIRD

Third basemen often have one of the strongest throwing arms on a baseball team. That's because they have to throw all the way across the diamond to beat runners down the first base line to record outs.

Third basemen often play close to the third-base bag, especially when an **opponent** has a runner on third base. They also might field bunts down the third base line, which doesn't give them much time to make a good throw to a base. This means third basemen often make off-balance throws in a hurry. If they're not **accurate**, the throw could miss the first baseman and be scored an **error**!

THE HOT CORNER

Third base is called the "hot corner" because third basemen usually play closer to the batter than anyone else in the field. Hits to this position often come very quickly off right-handed batters. A third baseman needs to have quick **reflexes** to not only catch potential hits for outs, but also stay safe!

THIRD BASEMEN NEED TO HAVE FAST REFLEXES AND THE ABILITY TO JUMP. SOMETIMES BALLS ARE HARD HIT JUST OVER THE THIRD BASEMAN'S HEAD. THEY CAN SNAG THEM IN THEIR GLOVE BEFORE THE BALLS REACH THE OUTFIELD AS HITS.

INFIELD CAPTAIN

Shortstops are some of the best athletes on the field. They must cover the most area on the infield, usually playing between second and third bases. The shortstop often turns double plays at second base and tells other infielders where to position themselves on the field for certain batters.

The shortstop usually covers second base when a catcher throws to the bag on a stolen base attempt. They can also quietly cover the bag for a pick-off attempt, or when a pitcher throws to second to catch a runner off the bag instead of throwing to home plate!

THE NUMBERS GAME

Fielding positions are often referred to by a number. The shortstop is number 6, after the pitcher, catcher, and first, second, and third basemen. The left fielder is 7, center fielder is 8, and right fielder is number 9. When outs are recorded in a scorebook, scorers use position numbers to track who made the out!

THE BEST FIELDER ON A TEAM IS OFTEN THE SHORTSTOP. THEY HAVE TO BE FAST, HAVE GOOD REFLEXES, AND HAVE A GREAT ARM. IT'S A HARD POSITION TO PLAY!

THE OUTFIELD

Now that we've covered the infield, let's get to the players standing furthest away from the batter. These are called outfielders. There are three different outfield positions: left fielder, center fielder, and right fielder. Their names come from where they stand in the outfield.

Center field is considered the hardest of these positions. Center fielders cover the most area in the outfield, so they have to be fast and able to make diving catches to stop hits. All outfielders are expected to have strong arms so they can make long throws back to the infield to keep runners from moving on the bases.

FLY BALL!

Catching a fly ball in the outfield is no easy task. Outfielders have to read the path of a ball to get under it and catch it with their glove. They sometimes battle sunlight and the wind to track a fly ball. Sometimes, more than one player might be tracking a ball. Fielders might need to call off their teammates to say they got it!

THE BEST OUTFIELD ARMS CAN THROW A BASEBALL HUNDREDS OF FEET IN THE AIR TO AN INFIELDER TO TAG A RUNNER OUT. VLADIMIR GUERRERO HAD A GREAT ARM, AND HE WAS VERY ACCURATE WITH HIS THROWS, TOO!

349 FT

COVERING THE GAPS

No batter tries to hit a ball to fielders. Instead, they try to find gaps in the defense. The gaps between the left fielder and center fielder and between the center fielder and right fielder are often called power alleys. If a player hits a ball to these alleys, they can run the bases for a double or even a triple.

Catching a runner trying to stretch a single into a double is a big job for an outfielder. Outfielders also need to back up another fielder trying to make a diving play on a ball in case they miss it. If a ball gets through an outfielder and reaches the outfield fence, a fast base runner can score!

Infielders and outfielders have to work together to get hit balls back into the infield quickly. Sometimes outfielders will throw to infielders who have moved out into the outfield to relay the ball back in faster than a long, slower throw. This infield player is called the cutoff, and their job is to quickly catch the outfielder's throw, turn, and then throw the ball to a base to keep a runner from moving up.

A HOME RUN WHERE A BATTER REACHES HOME WITHOUT HITTING THE BALL OVER THE FENCE IS CALLED AN INSIDE-THE-PARK HOME RUN!

GET IN THE GAME

Now that you know the basics of baseball, it's time for the advanced class. Did you know that, depending on where a ball is hit, position players need to move to cover certain bases?

If a first baseman tracks down a ground ball between first and second base, for example, the pitcher needs to cover first base to catch the ball and get the out! The catcher also runs up the first base line just in case the throw from the first baseman gets past the pitcher.

That's just one case of knowing your position in baseball. Keep watching and playing to pick up more tips to become a baseball **expert** yourself!

THE SHIFT

Forget everything you know about where fielders play when a manager breaks out "The Shift." This is a special move where fielders play different positions based on who is batting. Some left-handed hitters will see a third baseman shift over to play shortstop, who shifts to play between first and second while the second baseman plays shallow right field!

KNOWING WHERE TO GO AND WHAT TO DO IN BASEBALL TAKES LOTS OF PRACTICE. LISTEN TO YOUR COACHES AND WATCH THE PROS TO SEE HOW THEY PLAY THE GAME TO LEARN MORE!

GLOSSARY

accurate: free from mistakes; able to hit the target

athletic: strong and able to play a sport a long time at a high level

crouch: to stoop or bend low with the arms and legs close to the body

determine: to decide

error: a mistake made by a fielding player that allows a batter to reach base or a runner to advance

expert: someone who knows a great deal about something

opponent: a member of the other team in a game

reflexes: the ability to act quickly

statistic: facts that can be related in numbers

stolen base: a play in baseball where a base runner advances to another base, but not on a hit or walk

umpire: the person in charge of calling balls and strikes and making other rulings in a baseball game

wild pitch: a pitch thrown by a pitcher that isn't near the strike zone and could get past the catcher behind the plate

FOR MORE INFORMATION

BOOKS

Bryant, Howard. *Legends: The Best Players, Games, and Teams in Baseball.* New York, NY: Puffin Books, 2015.

Omoth, Tyler. *First Source to Baseball: Rules, Equipment, and Key Playing Tips.* North Mankato, MN: Capstone Press, 2016.

Yomtov, Nelson. *Being Your Best at Baseball.* New York, NY: Children's Press, 2017.

WEBSITES

Baseball Basics: On the Field
mlb.mlb.com/mlb/official_info/baseball_basics/on_the_field.jsp
Scroll over this interactive graphic to learn more about each position in baseball.

Baseball Glossary
m.mlb.com/glossary
Read all about special terms used in baseball and what they mean here.

Major League Baseball 2016 Official Rules
mlb.mlb.com/mlb/official_info/official_rules/official_rules.jsp
Learn more about the rules of baseball on the official Major League Baseball website.

INDEX